GET THEIR NAME

Grow Your Church
by Building New Relationships

Coordinator's Guide

Bob Farr
Kay Kotan

Abingdon Press™

Nashville

GET THEIR NAME COORDINATOR'S GUIDE:
GROW YOUR CHURCH BY BUILDING NEW RELATIONSHIPS

Copyright © 2016 by Abingdon Press

ISBN 978-1-5018-2543-9

Scripture quotations unless noted otherwise are from the Common English Bible. Copyright © 2011 by the Common English Bible. All rights reserved. Used by permission. www.CommonEnglishBible.com.

Scripture quotations from *The Message*. Copyright © by Eugene H. Peterson 1993, 1994, 1995, 1996, 2000, 2001, 2002. Used by permission of NavPress Publishing Group.

Our thanks to Christie Latona, Cathy Bien, the Baltimore-Washington Conference, and The United Methodist Church of the Resurrection for their generosity in sharing video content for this study.

16 17 18 19 20 21 22 23 24 25—10 9 8 7 6 5 4 3 2 1

MANUFACTURED IN THE UNITED STATES OF AMERICA

GET THEIR NAME: GROW YOUR CHURCH BY BUILDING NEW RELATIONSHIPS

A STUDY AND WORSHIP PLAN FOR OUTWARD-REACHING CONGREGATIONS

Congratulations! You have taken the first step in helping your church grow by building new relationships with new people. This study and sermon series, based on the book *Get Their Name: Grow Your Church by Building New Relationships*, is designed to help your congregation first understand why just inviting people to church is no longer an effective way to reach the unchurched. Secondly, it is designed to give your congregation the tools they individually and collectively need in order to build new relationships with new people. These concepts may be very new or different for some in your congregation. Lead with grace, but also with high expectations for all. After all, Matthew 28:19 calls for all our churches to make new disciples of Jesus Christ for the transformation of the world. This study is designed to help congregations and Christians do just that!

When an entire congregation engages in a shared topic for study, and it is coupled with the weekly sermon series, the opportunity for enormous momentum is created. When everyone is on the same page, everyone is moving, thinking, praying, and studying all in the same direction. When the church illustrates a collaborative effort, it allows the Holy Spirit to move more freely and readily. If you have some existing groups push back on joining the study, you might help bring them along when they understand this possibility.

May you be blessed as you lead your congregation on this journey to reach new people for Jesus Christ!

CONTENTS

PLANNING

In order to have a successful sermon series and congregational study, planning ahead is essential. The larger your church is, the more time you will most likely need for planning and promoting. *Get Their Name* is designed to help create a new culture of being an invitational church. The more planning and congregational participation you have, the greater chance you have of beginning to create a new invitational culture. Make sure you select an optimal season in the life of the church to conduct this congregational study and sermon series to gain the most momentum and participation. You might consider conducting this series as part of Lent or Advent. Or you might consider it as a fall or spring series.

When recruiting your group leaders, there are a few things you might want to consider.

First, be sure to include a variety of people (age, tenure, spiritual maturity, gender, etc.).

Second, make sure your leaders are able to offer a variety of times (daytime during the week, weekday evenings, during Sunday school, maybe Saturday morning, etc.).

Third, offer enough groups so that everyone has the opportunity to participate. Group sizes are best at around six to twelve people.

Fourth, encourage Sunday school classes or other ongoing small groups to participate. They could use the materials during their regular meeting time, or they could include a second meeting time if they want to continue with their current study but add this study, too. If the existing class or group does not choose to use the materials, suggest that the class leaders encourage their members to join another group for the four weeks at a time that does not conflict with their existing group. Consider challenging your congregation to reach a certain number of group participants.

Fifth, be prepared to resource group leaders whose groups choose to continue the small group experience after this study. They may enjoy their time and study so much that they don't want it to end! Be prepared to help them consider next steps in sustaining and equipping.

Small group leaders will need to know their faith story, so part of your training and equipping will be to help these leaders discover or refine their story. Small group participants will want to hear an example of a faith story, so the group leader will need to be prepared to share his or her story in order to encourage their participants to discover their own. Help your leaders work on this as you prepare them to lead.

The suggestions and steps described here are best practices. Some churches will have the resources to implement every step. Others will not. Implement as many of the steps as possible, but if you can't, don't let them intimidate you and keep you from conducting the series. Adapt the steps as needed for your church and its resources. Do the very best that you can. Stretch yourself a bit if needed, but don't overwhelm yourself in the process.

Remember, this study is only the first step. This is the equipping piece of the process—step one. Your church will also need to provide the next two steps in closing the gap on evangelism. Step two is helping the congregation understand the importance of evangelism—the "why." The third step is the action step—the practicing, going, and doing.

Think about what opportunities you might include during this study, immediately after, and in the upcoming year to emphasize the importance of being an invitational church and create opportunities for people to practice and implement the plan. People will be in various stages of their learning and confidence in implementing the steps, so be sure to create opportunities for a variety of levels. If possible, offer a servant evangelism opportunity during the study or right afterwards, since this is the first step in learning and practicing evangelism. If possible, ask some of your groups (new ones, already existing ones, and ministry teams) to begin to share their faith stories. If someone is ready, think about the possibility of having someone share his or her faith story in worship. If you have some people who really "get it," have them apprentice others by taking them out in the community to start conversations and build relationships in the mission field.

SUGGESTED TIMELINES

We have provided a suggested timeline and best practices for your consideration for planning purposes once you have the study and sermon dates on the church calendar. Larger churches may need more ramp-up time for certain tasks. Adapt the list to fit your local context and needs. You will need all resources (*Coordinator's Guide, Participant Workbooks*, and DVD of video clips) in hand before implementing the steps below.

Three Months Ahead

Gather a prayer team together to pray for this study, the participants, your pastor, and the unchurched in your community; also pray that the sermon series and study will result in reaching new people for Christ.

Gather small group leaders for planning and equipping.

Gather the worship design team & AV together to plan for series.

Gather the music team and worship leaders together to plan for series.

Gather the promotion team for creative planning.

Note: Those involved in leading (e.g., coordinator, pastor, small group facilitators, worship leader, staff, promotion team) need to read the original book *Get Their Name: Grow Your Church by Building New Relationships*.

Best practice would be for those leading to also work through the individualized questions in the *Workbook*.

Two Months Ahead

Begin to use the teaser promotion.

Make sure you have a variety of times and days available for small groups.

Meet with adult Sunday school teachers and invite them to join in by using the group study during their class time for four weeks.

One Month Ahead

Begin official promotion and group sign-ups.

Set the vision for everyone to be in a four-week group.

Pastor uses sermon outlines to prepare the message.

Worship design team is in final prep stages.

Music team is practicing music.

Prayer team continues to meet regularly to pray.

Print the steps to relational evangelism cards to be handed out to the congregation in week one.

One Week Ahead

Ensure everyone has had an opportunity to sign up for a group.

Call those who have not yet signed up to invite into a group.

Check in with pastor, music team and worship leaders, and worship design team on final preparations.

During Series

Check in with group facilitators.

Encourage and support group facilitators, pastor, music team and worship leaders, and worship design team on their participation and execution.

Evaluate execution weekly and make changes as needed.

After Series

Gather worship leaders and group facilitators to evaluate: What went well? What didn't? What did we learn? How might we incorporate our learnings in the future? Next steps?

Celebrate!

What's next? How will we continue to build an invitational culture? In worship? In small groups? In leadership?

Might you consider going deeper by offering the ten-week class using the full, ten-week Get Their Name Workbook? Have at least the Evangelism Team and Council participate.

Encourage leadership (e.g., pastor, staff, and council) to evaluate. What changes might we want to make in order to grow our church by reaching new people? Consider actions such as the following:

- Sharing faith stories in small groups
- Sharing our faith in worship
- Practicing servant evangelism
- Encouraging and supporting new relationships in the community with our radar engaged

After Series, continued

Also evaluate ways the church might focus on an invitational culture through use of the following:

- Church signage (inside and out)
- Church hospitality
- Guest friendly website
- Connection process
- Discipleship process for new people
- Ongoing outwardly focused prayer team
- Leadership development process
- Strategic ministry planning

PROMOTION

Proper and timely promotion will not only increase awareness of the upcoming series but it will also increase participation. Promotion will increase excitement and momentum. Have fun with it! This can be a scary or intimidating topic for some, so the lighter the mood, the higher the probability of participation.

You will want to gather your promotional team (or create one if you don't already have one). This team will include those working on the website, newsletter, bulletin, congregational e-mails, Facebook (and/or other social media), worship AV, drama team, graphic designer, and so on. You don't necessarily need a separate person for each of these duties. This is just a checklist of methods you might consider using to promote this study. Analyze the talents and resources in your church and gather what makes sense for your church. Jot down a list of people you think should be a part of this team:

Ideally the team providing the promotion should begin gathering at least three months in advance. This will give everyone time to plan, prepare, and execute without feeling rushed. This lead time will also provide the best quality promotion, execution, and participation. The team will focus on two different elements:

1. Creating excitement about the upcoming sermon series.

2. Promoting participation in small groups.

About two months prior to the study launch, your team will want to start "teasing" the congregation about the upcoming series. Make sure you are using multiple modes of communication on a weekly basis. Not everyone will be in worship, so make sure you offer alternative means of communication. Here are some ideas for your consideration to "tease" the congregation. Don't limit your imagination to just this list. It may only serve as an idea starter. Let your imagination run wild! Have fun with it! Use the book *Get Their Name* as a resource.

Find funny videos about "goofy" ways to evangelize and use the big circle with the line through it showing this is NOT the way we reach new people. Or design a skit that would illustrate how NOT to evangelize in today's culture.

Interview people in your congregation about what scares them or makes them feel uncomfortable about evangelism. Use people's fears in either a video or article to promote how we will help remove the fear about reaching new people.

Find stats on how many people are unchurched in today's world (e.g., pewresearch.org). Write an article and/or show a slide in worship with this information. Then challenge the congregation to think about what we must do to reach them since this is the mission of the church.

Design a skit with ten people out and about in a daily setting. Have another "churched" person learning about the ten people through conversation—how approximately seven of the ten are unchurched and why. Matthew 28 calls churches to make disciples, yet approximately seven of ten people are not disciples. How will our church reach the unchurched in our community?

If your church has been in decline, interview someone from the congregation that remembers the heyday of a bygone era.

- Ask them about the number of children or young families that were around.

- Ask them about how the activity level might be different today than back then.

- Ask them why they believe we are no longer reaching new people.

- Ask them what they think about evangelism in today's culture. How do we do it? What works? What doesn't? Have we seen fruits of our evangelism efforts in the past couple of years? If not, why? If so, how?

Use the interview in an article or video. This should illustrate that in bygone days, people came to us—the church. But in today's culture, we must go out and build relationships first and then bring them back with us to the gathered community.

Design a skit of an evangelism team or the pastor trying to recruit an evangelism team. Have people talk about all the "icky" thoughts/feelings/experiences that usually go along with the idea of evangelism. Have fun with this! Make it light-hearted. Finish the skit up with the message, "If you have these same thoughts and feelings about evangelism, stay tuned for how we might be able to reach new people in 'weird-free ways.' You won't want to miss the sermon series. Be sure to sign up for a small group."

Create so much buzz about the series and small groups that people won't want to "miss out" on what everyone else will be experiencing.

Talk about this as an opportunity for people who are not engaged in Sunday school or another group to get involved and "sample" small group community. This is short term—only four weeks. It is a chance to meet new friends and maybe try new desserts. It is a "taste and see" opportunity for small groups—it is a short commitment.

Have your pastor, staff member, or someone else write an article describing why they decided to participate in this study. What do they hope will occur as a result of this study? What participation do they dream about having within the congregation? How will this study influence the community in which the church resides?

Think about having the youth participate in some of the ideas above. Or ask them about ideas they might have about promoting the series.

Make sure you place information about the upcoming series and small group experiences using the newsletter, the bulletin, the screen, e-mail blasts, a phone campaign, Facebook, and so on. First it will be "coming soon," "watch for," and "you won't want to miss" messages. Then a month out, the messages will change to "sign up," "don't be left out," "only one week left to join," and so on.

Jot down the ideas from the suggestions above, and some of your own, that you'll pursue in order to promote the Get Their Name experience for your congregation:

RESOURCES

See bobfarr.org, gettheirname.com, or cokesbury.com for downloadable resources to use in implementing the study with your church. These resources include the following:

The 5-10-Link Card from *Clip In*, by Jim Ozier

WEAVE Card from *Clip In*, by Jim Ozier

Invitation

Six Steps to Relational Evangelism Card

Video Promos to show in worship and to share via social media

Graphics for use in worship and for customizing print and video promotional media

Downloadable Tips and Helps for Facilitating the *Get Their Name* Group Study (for distribution to small group facilitators)

WORSHIP DESIGN TEAM

The purpose of the worship design team is to fully prepare and create a meaningful worship experience that provides opportunities for people to experience the Holy Spirit during worship as God moves, shifts, and opens their eyes to a new way of reaching people. You will want to create these experiences through all the senses. Draw on ideas in the following areas: music, prayer, sermon, altar decorations, other chancel props, video, still images, handouts, drama, and scripture.

This *Coordinator's Guide* provides suggested scripture, prayers, songs, and sermon outlines for this series. Remember, there will be small groups gathering to go deeper into the topics each week, so not only is the team creating a worship experience, it is providing a springboard for the small group experience. Hopefully this is the beginning of a congregational cultural shift to become more outwardly focused to reach new people for Christ.

Following, you will find some idea starters for each week based on the sermon and scripture. Song suggestions are listed in the overview on pages 30–34. Videos for sermons and worship will be available online at bobfarr.org, gettheirname.com, and cokesbury.com. These will be useful to illustrate the main ideas in each sermon, or for emphasizing the sermon theme in another part of the worship service.

Each week, we will offer ideas on a physical takeaway for your congregation. These will serve as reminders of the message for the week and help to promote action as a result of the message.

WORSHIP OVERVIEW FOR DESIGN TEAM

SERIES TITLE SUGGESTIONS

Back to the Basics – Church Edition

How to Reach New People

Going Out Together

Sharing My Story, Your Story, Our Story

Why Church?

Building Relationships for Real Life

WEEK ONE: DO YOU KNOW YOUR OWN STORY?

<u>Scripture:</u> "So how can they call on someone they don't have faith in? And how can they have faith in someone they haven't heard of? And how can they hear without a preacher?" Romans 10:14

For week one, the idea is to help people think about evangelism in a new way. Evangelism is building relationships with people we don't know. The teaching is on faith sharing in groups and faith sharing in worship. Participants will work on developing and communicating their own faith stories.

We suggest opening the sermon with a video or story about evangelism done badly or awkwardly. Jot down your ideas for sermon openers here:

For your chancel area and altar, consider using items that are meaningful in people's faith journey. Jot down your ideas for chancel and altar decor here:

Hand out the "Steps to Relational Evangelism" card along with your bulletins. You can download the card here: bobfarr.org, gettheir name.com, and cokesbury.com. Another tangible take-away for your congregation is a pen for them to write their faith story so they can share it.

WEEK TWO: THE PERSON BEHIND THE NEED

<u>Scripture:</u> "As the lifeless body is dead, so faith without actions is dead." James 2:26

The overall theme for week two is to begin building relationships with people we now "serve." We are called to bring the Good News with the Good Deed. This might also be thought of as moving from "passive" service to "active, relational" service.

For the chancel area and altar, consider placing items that would remind us how we think about service. This could include food items (canned goods, boxed goods), tools (hammer, nails, and paint), clothing, blankets, shoes, socks, mittens, hats, and so on. If possible, how could faces (pictures or people) start appearing during the worship experience to reflect getting to know the people we serve? Jot down your ideas for chancel and altar decor. Also jot down ideas for showing faces of the people we serve.

A possible takeaway for the congregation would be a set of sunglasses to "see" people in a different way. Jot down other ideas for tangible takeaways:

WEEK THREE: BEING AN EVERYDAY CHRISTIAN

<u>Scripture:</u> "He replied, 'Come along and see for yourself.'" John 1:39 (*The Message*)

The theme for week three is how we build relationships with new people outside the church. This is about slowing down our fast-paced lives and "seeing" the people around us.

For the chancel area and altar, consider placing items that remind us of our everyday life. This might include a computer or briefcase, backpack, fast-food wrappers/bags, convenience-store cups, coffee-house cups, cash register or other things that remind us of where we shop, telephone, computer, and so on. Again, you could begin to include people among the "things" during the sermon. Jot down your ideas for chancel and altar decor. Try to include some ideas to represent people, too.

You could use still images of the blur of people rather than seeing the faces of the people around us. The blur could become more focused through worship. Jot down ideas for using imagery of people during worship.

A possible congregational takeaway is some sort of invitation in an envelope for congregants to invite someone to an event. It could be an invitation to church, but a best practice would be to invite them to an activity that might be less intimidating than worship (small group in home, social event, fun activity, etc.). See download: bobfarr.org, gettheirname.com, and cokesbury.com. Jot down ideas for an event, service activity, or other opportunity that you could invite people to with a printed invitation.

WEEK FOUR: ARE YOU PREPARED?

<u>Scripture:</u> "Don't neglect to open up your homes to guests, because by doing this some have been hosts to angels without knowing it." Hebrews 13:2

For week four, the theme is preparing our church to receive guests. Are we prepared for and anticipating the receiving of guests every week?

For the chancel area and altar, consider dressing the area as though you are receiving honored guests. Put out your best dinnerware, finest silver, and crystal. Include nice table linens, beautiful serving dishes, and elegant candelabras. Go all out in creating a beautiful display that demonstrates much planning and putting our best foot forward to receive honored guests. Jot down ideas for chancel and altar decor:

For a possible congregational takeaway, make cards (or download here) of Jim Ozier's 5-10-Link and WEAVE card (available at bobfarr .org, gettheirname.com, and cokesbury.com).

WORSHIP OVERVIEW FOR MUSIC TEAM AND WORSHIP LEADERS

Key:

UMH	*United Methodist Hymnal*
TFWS	*The Faith We Sing*
WS	*Worship and Song*

WEEK ONE: DO YOU KNOW YOUR OWN STORY?

Scripture: "So how can they call on someone they don't have faith in? And how can they have faith in someone they haven't heard of? And how can they hear without a preacher?" Romans 10:14

Song Suggestions:

I Know Whom I Have Believed - UMH #714

Go, Make of All Disciples - UMH #571

Pass It On - UMH #572

I Love to Tell the Story - UMH #156

As a Fire Is Meant for Burning - TFWS #2237

Spirit of God - TFWS #2117

Go to the World - WS #3158

In Christ Alone - WS #3105

Prayer: Oh God, you are the source of our wisdom. Fill us with your insight and understanding so that we might go into this broken world and share what you mean to each of us. Guide us with your Holy Spirit as we strive to be more Christlike. In Jesus's name we pray. Amen.

Benediction: Oh Inviting God, thank you for allowing us to experience you on a daily basis. Help us to have the eyes, ears, and heart to notice you each day. Then, Lord, give us the courage to share our stories with those you put in our path to hear it. In your Son's name we pray. Amen.

WEEK TWO: THE PERSON BEHIND THE NEED

Scripture: "As the lifeless body is dead, so faith without actions is dead." James 2:26

Song Suggestions:

> Many Gifts, One Spirit - UMH #114
>
> Here I Am, Lord - UMH #593
>
> Lord, Whose Love through Humble Service - UMH #581
>
> Pues Si Vivimos (When We Are Living) - UMH #356
>
> The Spirit Sends Us Forth to Serve - TFWS #2241
>
> The Servant Song - TFWS #2222
>
> Love the Lord - WS #3116

Prayer: Oh God, who goes before us, we seek you in this time of learning. Let your Holy Spirit surround each of us as we seek to hear and understand you today. Let our hearts and eyes be opened to see and experience the world as you would. In Jesus's name we pray. Amen.

Benediction: Oh loving and compassionate God, thank you for the stirrings in our hearts as you work in and through us. Help us to see those in our community that we help in a new light. May we notice, see, experience, and reach out to those whom we are called to serve. May we not only offer a helping hand, but also offer a relationship of love, hope, and grace. In your precious Son's name we pray. Amen.

WEEK THREE: BEING AN EVERYDAY CHRISTIAN

<u>Scripture</u>: "He replied, 'Come along and see for yourself.'" John 1:39 (*The Message*)

Song Suggestions:

> We've a Story to Tell to the Nations - UMH #569
>
> Lord, I Want to Be a Christian - UMH #402
>
> O Church of God, United - UMH #547
>
> Hymn of Promise - UMH #707
>
> They'll Know We Are Christians by Our Love - TFWS #2223
>
> Sanctuary - TFWS #2164

<u>Prayer</u>: Heavenly Father, we recognize the temptation to expect others to come to us, rather than us reaching out to others. Today, Lord, we seek to be a church that goes out into our mission field to build relationships with those who have yet to meet you. Lord, send your Holy Spirit to be with us as we seek to understand your way of reaching the unconnected and the disconnected. In Jesus's name we pray. Amen.

<u>Benediction</u>: Oh God of goodness and grace, slow us down in this fast-paced world. Help us to see those we encounter in our lives. Help us to engage with those we encounter. Help us to be bold and relentless in building relationships with those we encounter. And then, Heavenly Father, let us have an engaged radar so we respond with our faith stories when you have opened the door for us to do so. For God, we know you use us to reach your people. Let us recognize those opportunities to serve you. In your Son's name we pray. Amen.

WEEK FOUR: ARE YOU PREPARED?

<u>Scripture:</u> "Don't neglect to open up your homes to guests, because by doing this some have been hosts to angels without knowing it." Hebrews 13:2

Song Suggestions:

Help Us Accept Each Other - UMH #560

Jesus, United by Thy Grace - UMH #561

Jesu, Jesu - UMH #432

Let There Be Peace on Earth - UMH #431

Come, Now Is the Time to Worship - WS #3176

Shout to the North - WS #3042

Mighty to Save - WS #3038

<u>Prayer:</u> Father God, we seek you today. Pour your Holy Spirit over us as we prepare to receive your people. Let us be open to your movement as we see our church today through the eyes of guests. Help us first recognize and then be willing to remove our blind spots. Let us learn to demonstrate radical hospitality as you have instructed us to do. In your Son's name we pray. Amen.

<u>Benediction:</u> Loving God, help us prepare to receive your honored guests each and every Sunday. May we make ourselves available to offer not only friendliness but also radical hospitality and authentic relationship. May we be a place where guests feel comfort, peace, hope, and a sense of belonging. May we offer our guests meaningful connections with us and, more importantly, with you. Yes, company is a comin'. Let us be prepared with anticipation to receive them! In Jesus's name we pray. Amen.

Additional Song Suggestions for the Series:

    If We Are the Body - Mark Hall

    What Did He Die For - Twila Paris

    Thrive - Matthew West & Mark Hall

    Voice of Truth - Mark Hall & Steven Curtis Chapman

    Hope in Front of Me - Danny Gokey

    My Story - Big Daddy Weave

Jot down the ideas you have for other songs to use during this series. Also write down ideas from others in the music and worship ministry.

SERMON OUTLINES

SERMON NOTES

Following are suggested outlines to help guide you with content based on the teachings from the book. Depending on the length of time you have to preach, you may or may not be able to make it through the entire outline. This is simply a starting point for your consideration and assistance. Please make it your own. You might also like to find some characters in the Bible to use as illustrations to bring the teachings to life and align a more personal and identifiable moment for your congregants (e.g., Mary and Martha for week four). Tailor it so that you are comfortable and authentic while covering the major points. You can use these during the sermon, another time in the worship order, or a combination.

WEEK ONE: DO YOU KNOW YOUR OWN STORY?

I. Explain why evangelism in the modern church gets a bad rap.

    a. Possible illustrations: a personal story, experience, or video to illustrate evangelism done badly (forceful, convicting, harmful, judgmental, etc.) Other ideas for opening illustrations:

    b. Trying vs. Training

      i. Sometimes we just keep trying the same old things and expect a new outcome.

      ii. Evangelism is building authentic relationships with people you do not know.

      iii. We need training!

II. Two Components of Evangelism

    a. Witness: service, building, light of Christ

    b. Inviting: invitation to others to experience God

      i. This example points to John the Baptist—"come and see" (John 1:39). He replied, "Come along and see for yourself." They came and saw where he was living and ended up staying with him for the day.

      ii. Thirty years ago we pointed to the church. Today we need to point to our experience of God.

III. Learn your own story!

  a. The power of a recommendation

    i. Share a personal story about how you recommended or received a recommendation on a product, service, or experience. Ideas for personal story/illustration:

    ii. When we think about recommending as it relates to our faith, we most likely recommend the church. People couldn't care less about your church. They want to first know you care and then why God would care.

  b. Four steps in training yourself to tell your story:

    i. Faith sharing in service

      1. Stay tuned next week to hear about this one

    ii. Faith sharing in a safe group

      1. Tell me about a time *lately* you have experienced God.

      2. Start in small groups, safe places.

      3. Faith story = elevator speech

a. Adam Hamilton's Questions

- Why God?
- Why Church?
- Why Your Church?

4. As you think about your story, remember Jesus's style of evangelism:

   a. Conversation not confrontation

   b. Invitation rather than invasion

   c. Adventure rather than argument

   d. Experience rather than a stand

   e. Personal discovery rather than vigorous debate

5. Jesus's style of evangelism is people-loving and life-giving.

6. It is in the everyday, ordinary moments of our lives.

iii. Faith sharing in worship

1. It is important for the community of faith that some people other than preachers get the courage up to share their testimonies.

2. Testimony is typically a very short story about where you met God in some experience recently.

3. We are most acquainted with this as a camp story or a mission trip experience story.

   a. We expect our kids to come back from camp and share their story and others to come back from mission trips and share their stories, yet we do not share our story about meeting God in ordinary everyday places.

4. In his preaching journeys, Francis Asbury always brought along a layperson to share their experience.

5. Share a video about someone else sharing their story. Who in your congregation might tell about how they've shared their faith, on video or in some other format? List ideas here:

    iv. Faith sharing with uncommitted
        1. We'll talk about this one in week three.

IV. Call to action: ask congregants to consider these questions:

- What step are you on in learning your story?

- What is your next step?

- Are you noticing the God moments in your life?

- Where are you practicing your story?

- Wherever you are—at the beginning, the middle, or a pro— do you know your faith story?

Write ideas for biblical characters, stories, or other scriptural references to use in this sermon:

WEEK TWO: THE PERSON BEHIND THE NEED

I. Idea for introductory video: Create a video showing different people trying on each other's eyeglasses and their funny reactions to seeing through someone else's lenses. Other ideas for opening illustrations:

II. We are all called to service.

  a. "For the Human One didn't come to be served but rather to serve and to give his life to liberate many people" (Mark 10:45 CEB).

III. Celebrate the ways your church already serves others people. List your ideas here:

IV. But what is service?

    a. We do lots of good deeds, but where are places that we can also spread the Good News?

    b. How do we follow the green beans, warm coat, and blankets to the recipient?

        i. Get their name.

        ii. Build a relationship.

        iii. Share our faith story.

        iv. Bring them with us back to the gathered community of faith.

    c. Give an example using a service project that could be turned into a relationship opportunity too. List ideas here:

V. Mission Trips

    a. Celebrate the missions in which your church participates. List ideas here:

    b. There is normally a "task" to be completed that precipitates the trip (storm recovery, building new houses, teachings VBS, etc.).

    c. We tend to focus on the "task" at hand.

    d. We busy ourselves with work, but sometimes we miss the relational opportunities.

e. The true focus is not really the task—it is the relationship between the participants and the receivers.

VI. Blessings

a. Be kind (open doors, smile, say hello, etc.).

b. Compliment (clothing, children, car, behavior, deed, etc.).

c. Engage people with your eyes and words when conducting transactions (for example, at the grocery store, gas station, bank, dry cleaners, etc.).

d. "Notice" people around you at a deeper level (take off blinders, engage radar).

VII. Deeper Needs

a. We are mostly quick to notice basic needs (food, shelter, clothing).

b. We often miss seeing the deeper needs (such as those related to loneliness, depression, financial balance, parenting, relationships, self-esteem, marriage, job, or stress).

c. By seeing, responding, and building relationships with people with deeper needs, we have a greater chance of not only helping but also being used to help them find God.

VIII. Review

a. We must balance our service work with the opportunity to engage people in relationship (moving from passive to active service).

b. We must see our service as people and not tasks—we are in the "people business."

c. Call to action: ask congregants to consider these questions during the upcoming days.

   i. How might God be calling you to see the people behind the needs in our community?

ii. What is one step you would consider in building a relationship with those we are helping?

Write ideas for biblical characters, stories, or other scriptural references to use in this sermon:

WEEK THREE: BEING AN EVERYDAY CHRISTIAN

I. Idea for introductory video: Create a video showing people in your church. Include people in worship, fellowship, Sunday school, or other activities that are typical inside the walls of your own congregation. Other ideas for opening illustrations:

II. We must move from a **come in** movement to a **go out** movement.

    a. People won't just show up at the doors—it's countercultural in today's world.

    b. See statistics on page 1 of *Get Their Name*. Write the stats or other information that are most compelling for your congregation here:

    c. We are going to have to learn to become twenty-first-century missionaries.

III. So how do we do this without being "weird"?

    a. Remember: we are missionaries.

        i. Not just on Sunday or on mission trips

        ii. EVERYDAY

    b. Have an intentional plan.

    i.   How much time are you spending with the un-connected?

    ii.   Who in your F.R.A.N. (friends, relatives, acquaintances, neighbors) circle is unconnected?

    iii.   Work in your normal affinities—with your radar engaged!

    iv.   "Walking along the beach of Lake Galilee, Jesus saw two brothers: Simon (later called Peter) and Andrew. They were fishing, throwing their nets into the lake. It was their regular work. Jesus said to them, 'Come with me. I'll make a new kind of fisherman out of you. I'll show you how to catch men and women instead of perch and bass.' They didn't ask questions, but simply dropped their nets and followed" (Matthew 4:18-20 *The Message*).

  c. Work outside your comfort zone.

    i.   Make new friends in new places.

    ii.   Create new hangout places; connect with mutual friends; see people; offer blessings.

    iii.   "Just then his disciples came back. They were shocked. They couldn't believe he was talking with that kind of a woman. No one said what they were all thinking, but their faces showed it" (John 4:27 *The Message*).

IV. How do you move from an acquaintance to authentic relationship?

  a. "The Samaritan woman, taken aback, asked, 'How come you, a Jew, are asking me, a Samaritan woman, for a drink?' (Jews in those days wouldn't be caught dead talking to Samaritans.)" (John 4:9 *The Message*).

  b. Begin with friendship.

  c. Listen for their story.

  d. Watch for signals.

  e. Use bridge-building phrase.

    f. Know your story.

    g. Find need and connect to new people with new people.

    h. Trust the Spirit.

V. It's All about Relationships

    a. It is still true that the majority of people find God because of other people.

    b. Call to action: Ask congregants to consider these questions over the next several days.

      i. What's your plan?

      ii. God uses us to reach new people. How are you showing up for his work?

Write ideas for biblical characters, stories, or other scriptural references to use in this sermon:

WEEK FOUR: ARE YOU PREPARED?

I. Idea for introductory video: Create a video showing a person, couple, or family preparing to have guests over for dinner. Show them cleaning, tidying, preparing food, setting the table, adding flowers or other decorations, sweeping the front porch, and so on. If you want to give the video a humorous tone, speed up the video so that it is in fast motion, and add frenetic music. Other ideas for opening illustrations:

II. Relationships Matter: Guest vs. Visitor

    a. Do you remember a time when you were looking forward to receiving company at your home?

    b. Give personal example (talk about why you were excited, preparations, great time you had). Ideas for your personal example:

    c. On the contrary, do you remember a time when someone dropped by unexpectedly (not prepared, didn't expect, didn't have time, upset your schedule)?

    d. First example is a guest. Second example is a visitor.

    i. Guests are invited; we expect them, make special preparations, look forward to them.

    ii. Visitors are not expected; we aren't prepared, and we don't necessarily look forward to them.

    iii. Do we have visitors drop by our church, or are we preparing, inviting, and anticipating guests each and every Sunday?

III. Friendly vs. Friendship

  a. We are a friendly church (say only if true!), but are we only friendly to one another? Or are we also friendly to guests?

  b. How would a guest perceive our church culture?

    i. Open, intentional, relational, ability to break into groups, ability to belong? OR...

    ii. Family reunion, friendly but not open to relationships, cliques, into one another more than receiving new people?

    iii. Give example of someone going to a family reunion. Don't know stories, customs, traditions, names, and so on. Feel out of place. List ideas of a personal example or an example from someone else's real life:

IV. Elements of Welcoming Our Guests

    a. Three touches before getting to seat in worship (parking lot, exterior door, sanctuary door)

    b. Hospitality (meeting common expectations) vs. radical hospitality (above & beyond)

    c. Connector (host, intro to others, pastor intro, next steps, get name, follow-up)

    d. Connection process (day of, day after, and until person finds a place and sticks beyond worship)

    e. Faith development process, not membership (how do we go from guest to connected to new believer to disciple to missionary/ambassador?)

V. Building Matters

    a. How would you rate our facility on guest friendliness?

       i. Road sign and parking

      ii. Door signage

     iii. Interior signage (restrooms, worship, children)

     iv. Information (digital bulletin boards, ministry & service opportunities, next steps)

      v. Nursery (nearest room to worship area, clean, well staffed, check in/out, modern & safe furnishings, trained staff)

     vi. Hospitality area at front door (coffee, food, refreshments, fellowship)

    vii. The first facility most guests encounter: your website

        1. How are we doing?

        2. Guest friendly?

        3. Know what to expect as a guest?

        4. Up to date?

        5. Worship info on front page?

        6. Pictures of ministries and staff?

VI. Leadership Matters

    a. Our church can only grow to the degree that we raise up new leaders.

    b. These leaders need to be spiritually mature people who are about the mission of making disciples.

    c. We must plan strategically and missionally to align what we do with the mission of making disciples.

    d. We must be about equipping our congregation to live missionally.

VII. Review

    a. Relationships Matter—preparation and expectation of receiving guests each Sunday

    b. Building Matters—first impression and how we function/what we value

    c. Leadership Matters—We must be led by leaders who are enthusiastic about our mission of reaching new people.

Write ideas for biblical characters, stories, or other scriptural references to use in this sermon:

APPENDIX

The following resources are for your reference. The section titled Tips and Helps for Facilitating the *Get Their Name* Group Study should be distributed to all facilitators of the small groups in the early stages of planning and equipping. The Tips and Helps are also available for free download online at bobfarr.org, gettheirname.com, and cokesbury.com.

The Participant Workbook included here is a condensed version of the *Get Their Name Participant Workbook* that each participant in the groups will use during the four-week study. This material is for your reference as you plan coordinating events during the weeks of the study.

TIPS AND HELPS FOR FACILITATING THE *GET THEIR NAME* GROUP STUDY

Thank you for your willingness to facilitate a group study of *Get Their Name*. This experience is sure to be a blessing for you and for the participants. Facilitating this study is pretty simple. Your primary tasks are to prepare the space for each session, show the video conversation starters, and help your group engage in meaningful conversation in a positive environment.

The group sessions will typically run 60–90 minutes.

Someone in your congregation—perhaps you!—will be serving as the overall coordinator of your church's *Get Their Name* experience. The coordinator will likely organize people into groups, arrange for meeting spaces, and attend to other organizational details. Make sure to **communicate with your coordinator.**

You may want to have snacks or a meal as part of your time together. If you choose to do this, be sure to plan this time in addition to the "study" time. On the other hand, don't feel like you need to provide snacks or a meal as part of your time together. You might check in with your participants ahead of time to determine their preferences. Or you might just set up expectations for your group ahead of time based on your own preferences as the facilitator. You might consider meeting outside the church—in homes or public places such as libraries, restaurants, parks, or office spaces.

To prepare, read the book *Get Their Name,* upon which this study is based. Familiarize yourself with the overall concepts. If you have questions about the material, or if questions arise during your group sessions that you cannot answer, talk with the coordinator or your pastor.

Encourage participants in your group to read the book too. Not only will they get more from your time together, but they will have an expanded understanding of how to grow your church by building new relationships. Note: an expanded workbook is also available. It is an in-depth chapter-by-chapter study of the original book. If your group or individuals in the group wish to go deeper, consider using this additional resource.

Each week's session follows this simple format:

1. Opening Prayer

2. Introduction (week one only)

- *Your name?*
- *Why did you choose to join the group?*
- *What do you hope to take away from this study?*

3. Review of Homework (after week one)

4. Read Scripture

5. Watch Video

6. Discussion Questions

7. Takeaway

8. Homework Assignment

9. Closing Prayer

Here are a few tips for facilitating the group study:

- *Clearly communicate the start time, end time, start date, end date, and location.*

- *Provide your contact information, and ask participants to let you know if they are unable to attend.*

- *Start on time. End on time.*

- *Be prepared to open and close each session in prayer yourself, but after the first week, ask for volunteers to offer the prayer too. Ask in advance, outside the meeting time, so participants don't feel pressured.*

- *Arrive in advance each week to prepare your meeting place, so that it is ready when participants arrive.*

- *Set up the DVD player, TV, or whatever technology you are using to play the video each week before participants arrive.*

- *Encourage participation from all. If you have someone who seems reluctant to speak, that person may be someone who internally processes. Or they may be a bit shy. Ask them questions to bring them into the group discussion, but don't put them on the spot in asking for a specific answer. Rather, you might ask if they might share a thought about a particular subject at hand.*

- *You are not required to have all the answers! Your job is to facilitate a meaningful, Spirit-filled conversation. So relax and enjoy!*

- *Facilitate conversation with open-ended questions. These often start with "What do you think about" or "Describe a time in your life when" or "Share what is most meaningful for you about," and so forth. Try not to use questions that can be answered with yes or no.*

- *Be an encourager, and keep the discussion on track. Participants may find some of the information and questions challenging. As the group wrestles with the lessons, allow people to share their struggles, but don't allow the session to be derailed. Acknowledge the struggles, and then bring the discussion back to the topic at hand.*

Set clear expectations for the group at your first meeting. Ask the group participants to

- arrive on time;

- complete the homework assignments;

- attend regularly, so that the group benefits from the variety of perspectives;

- be in prayer for one another for the duration of the study; and

- respect the different thoughts and opinions expressed in their time together. In these differences we see through an entirely new lens, which is beneficial and a desired result of the study. Your group should be rooted in grace and love for one another.

Thank you again for your willingness to serve! Remember, this is a chance for you to learn, engage, and wrestle with the materials too. May you and your group be blessed through this study. And through this study may your church grow by building new relationships with new people!

GET THEIR NAME
PARTICIPANT WORKBOOK

INTRODUCTION

Welcome! Thank you for your courage to embark on this journey with us and your group! This study is meant to stir and maybe even challenge you a bit; it is designed to take you and your group to a safe place to reflect, ask questions, wrestle with information, push back, and be accelerated forward with the help of the Holy Spirit. May your time together be a blessing!

This study is based on the book *Get Their Name: Grow Your Church by Building New Relationships*. You should read the book before you begin this study in order to fully participate. Each week, you will view a video that serves as both a teaching moment and your conversation starter.

Our approach for reaching new people may differ from the methods you are familiar with. We have found that most of us have been taught that to reach new people, we invite them to church. While this method may have once worked in a church-centric world, it is proving to be ineffective in our not-so-church-centric world today. So we must reach people in a new way. This resource was designed to help you do just that.

For best results, think of this study not only as information to be gained (head stuff), but also as a study of the heart. If you are open, this study is a potential paradigm shifter! Currently, church attendance is in decline. We must be willing to see the unchurched in our communities with a new lens, one that tugs at our hearts to be faithful to our purpose—to make disciples of Jesus Christ for the transformation of the world. We ask that you open yourselves up to learning and adapting to a new way of following Jesus Christ and being the church.

Use this workbook as your journal. Mark in it. Record answers to your questions along with thoughts, shifts, and questions that come up for you. Continue to look back at the questions and answers and see what God might continue to reveal to you. Take the time to work on your reflection questions between your group gatherings. This will allow you to reflect personally on the sermon, teachings, and conversation from your group.

Enjoy your journey discovering and refining your faith story throughout your time in this group!

You are the light of the world. A city on top of a hill can't be hidden. Neither do people light a lamp and put it under a basket. Instead, they put it on top of a lampstand, and it shines on all who are in the house. In the same way, let your light shine before people, so they can see the good things you do and praise your Father who is in heaven.

—Matthew 5:14-16

Week One

DO YOU KNOW YOUR OWN STORY?

OPENING PRAYER

Loving Father, we come to you today with open hearts and open minds. We ask that our time together be filled with the Holy Spirit and guided by you in our learning today. We are your clay; mold us into being your disciples to reach new people so that they may know and serve you. In Jesus's name we pray. Amen.

INTRODUCTIONS

- Your name?
- Why did you choose to join the group?
- What do you hope to take away from this study?

SCRIPTURE

Come close and listen,

all you who honor God;

I will tell you what God has done for me:

My mouth cried out to him

with praise on my tongue.

—Psalm 66:16-17

VIDEO PRESENTATION

Notes:

Group Discussion Questions

1. What is your first impression about the video? What intrigues you? Challenges you?

2. What is your faith story? Would you share it with the group? If you don't have one, how will you begin to develop yours? Where will you begin to practice sharing it in safe places?

3. How is your church doing at reaching new people on a regular basis?

4. How are you personally doing at engaging people in new relationships outside the church? What is working well? What are your challenges? Share a story about a new relationship.

5. Review the steps for relational evangelism listed below. Where are you doing well in the process? Where are you stuck? What might help you move to the next step?

GET THEIR
NAME _____ *Book Excerpt*

Six Steps to Relational Evangelism:

1. Listen for their story.
2. Watch for signals.
3. Use bridge-building phrases.
4. Know your elevator story.
5. Know your faith story.
6. Find the need and connect new people with new people.

—*Get Their Name*, pp. 57–65

KEY TAKEAWAY

_____

_____

_____

_____

_____

_____

_____

_____

HOMEWORK

Get names and start conversations with three new people this week. If you aren't comfortable with three, try two. In the upcoming week, answer the questions for personal reflection you see below. Next week, we will talk about our experiences with this homework.

CLOSING PRAYER

Father God, thank you for the presence of your Holy Spirit this evening as we begin to think about learning to articulate our faith stories. As we leave this place, Lord, help us to see you in our everyday lives. Help us to recognize your hand at work as we go about our days. And then, dear Lord, gives us the strength and courage to begin to start conversations with people who don't know you, so that we might be able to eventually share our faith story. In your Son's name we pray. Amen.

QUESTIONS FOR PERSONAL REFLECTION

1. Where am I most comfortable building new relationships and having the opportunity to share my story? Do I need to create new places? If so, where? When will I go?

2. What are obstacles that keep me from building new relationships, if any? How might I overcome them? Why is it important to overcome them?

3. What difference would it make in my life if I began to build relationships with new people and share my story? What difference might it make in the world?

Jesus answered, "Everyone who drinks this water will be thirsty again, but whoever drinks from the water that I will give will never be thirsty again. The water that I give will become in those who drink it a spring of water that bubbles up into eternal life." The woman said to him, "Sir, give me this water, so that I will never be thirsty and will never need to come here to draw water!"

—John 4:13-15

Week Two

THE PERSON BEHIND THE NEED

OPENING PRAYER

Oh, merciful and loving God, we seek you in our lives and our group today. As we work through our questions, urge us, encourage us, stretch us, and challenge us in seeing the unchurched in a new light. Help us to see all people as your people. Help us to take the step beyond serving to actually "being" with all your people. In Jesus's name we pray. Amen.

REVIEW OF HOMEWORK

1. Share about the new conversations you started with people you didn't know this past week. Where did you see God working in opening up those opportunities to start conversations?

2. What were some of the outcomes? Wins? Challenges?

3. What came up for you while working through your personal reflection questions?

SCRIPTURE

Therefore, go and make new disciples of all nations, baptizing them in the name of the Father and of the Son and of the Holy Spirit, teaching them to obey everything that I've commanded you. Look, I myself will be with you every day until the end of this present age.

—Matthew 28:19-20

VIDEO PRESENTATION

Notes:

Group Discussion Questions

1. What are your reflections on the video today? What intrigues you? What challenges you?

2. Why is it important to build relationships with those we serve?

3. What impact might we have as a church if we practice relationship building along with serving?

4. What would it take to shift this service into relational evangelism? What types of ministries create opportunities to build meaningful relationships that may lead to faith sharing?

5. Are there ministries we might have to stop in order to have the resources (time, energy, dollars, people) to practice servant evangelism (the heart of what God calls the church to do)? What are your thoughts about this?

GET THEIR
NAME

Relational Evangelism: Good Deed + Good Word = Good News

"Relational evangelism through service is connecting service to a clear . . . communication of the Good News of God's love."

—*Get Their Name*, p. 7

KEY TAKEAWAY

CLOSING PRAYER

Note: Part of becoming more comfortable in sharing our faith story is also learning to pray with and for others. For the rest of the sessions, take turns giving the closing prayer. This is great practice!

HOMEWORK

Spend time in prayer and reflection over the next week considering where your church might be able to shift current service opportunities into relationship-building opportunities. In the upcoming week, answer the questions for personal reflection you see below. Be prepared to share your thoughts next week.

QUESTIONS FOR PERSONAL REFLECTION

1. How are you doing with developing your faith story? What needs work? Who have you shared it with to practice? Are you ready to share it with a new person with whom you have developed a relationship when the appropriate time comes?

2. Where is a place that you can personally serve and also build a relationship?

3. What challenges you about this lesson? What excites you about this lesson?

4. How is the Holy Spirit working on you through this group study experience?

Jesus answered, "Everyone who drinks this water will be thirsty again, but whoever drinks from the water that I will give will never be thirsty again. The water that I give will become in those who drink it a spring of water that bubbles up into eternal life." The woman said to him, "Sir, give me this water, so that I will never be thirsty and will never need to come here to draw water!"

—John 4:13-15

Brothers and sisters, we ask you to respect those who are working with you, leading you, and instructing you. Think of them highly with love because of their work. Live in peace with each other. Brothers and sisters, we urge you to warn those who are disorderly. Comfort the discouraged. Help the weak. Be patient with everyone. Make sure no one repays a wrong with a wrong, but always pursue the good for each other and everyone else. Rejoice always. Pray continually. Give thanks in every situation because this is God's will for you in Christ Jesus. Don't suppress the Spirit. Don't brush off Spirit-inspired messages, but examine everything carefully and hang on to what is good.

—1 Thessalonians 5:12-21

Week Three

BEING AN EVERYDAY CHRISTIAN

OPENING PRAYER

Loving Father, we come to you today with open hearts and open minds. We admit that it is sometimes difficult for us to reach out to others and connect in a deep and meaningful way. Bless our conversations today; may you fill us with your Holy Spirit as we discuss how to be a Christian in today's world. In Jesus's name we pray. Amen.

REVIEW OF HOMEWORK

1. Reflect on your past week's thoughts and prayers. What missional opportunities does your church offer that naturally provide a chance to build relationships with those you serve?

2. How could you incorporate those next steps that lead to faith sharing? How might this happen? What is the first step?

3. In working through your personal reflection questions, what did you discover?

4. How is God working in you to learn and share your faith story better?

SCRIPTURE

Act wisely toward outsiders, making the most of the opportunity. Your speech should always be gracious and sprinkled with insight so that you may know how to respond to every person.

—Colossians 4:5-6

VIDEO PRESENTATION

Notes:

Group Discussion Questions

1. What are some things you might notice about a person that could potentially start a conversation (e.g., Harley motorcycles, Mustangs, vacation destination, handbag)?

2. How might one recognize a signal that a person is ready to take the next step in your relationship? Discuss some possible signals.

3. Discuss the three questions new people might ask: Why God? Why church? Why your church? How might you answer each one? Does this help you in refining your faith story?

KEY TAKEAWAY

_____

_____

_____

_____

_____

_____

_____

CLOSING PRAYER

Note: This week for the closing prayer, each person will participate. One person starts the prayer and then, going around the room, each person adds a sentence to the prayer. The last person closes the prayer.

HOMEWORK

Think and pray about who God is calling you to reach out to in order to form a new or deeper relationship. Write down three names in the space below. Pray in the upcoming week that God would provide the opportunity to take the next step with these three people. Share about your experience next week with your group.

Book Excerpt

F.R.A.N.:

Friends, Relatives, Acquaintances/Associates, and Neighbors

—*Get Their Name*, p. 48

QUESTIONS FOR PERSONAL REFLECTION

1. We know that the majority of people find God because of another person. Who is God placing on your heart to connect with either to start a new relationship or take the next step in a relationship that might lead to God?

2. If you find yourself thinking everyone you know is already Christian, where are some new places you might hang out or new groups you might join in order to build new relationships?

From now on, brothers and sisters, if anything is excellent and if anything is admirable, focus your thoughts on these things: all that is true, all that is holy, all that is just, all that is pure, all that is lovely, and all that is worthy of praise. Practice these things: whatever you learned, received, heard, or saw in us. The God of peace will be with you.

—Philippians 4:8-9

Week Four

ARE YOU PREPARED?

OPENING PRAYER

O Holy One, we come to you for guidance. At times, our church family is not as hospitable as we should be to those who visit your house of worship. Lord, help us to see our church through your eyes. Help us to see our church through the eyes of the unchurched so that we begin to prepare to receive your people as you, yourself would receive them. It is in Christ's name we pray. Amen.

REVIEW OF HOMEWORK

1. What names were placed on your heart to reach out to?

2. Did you pray for them? Were you afforded opportunities to start conversations with them? Share your experiences.

3. Talk about the places you currently hang out or where new opportunities to hang out might arise to start new relationships with new people. Who will hold you accountable for doing so?

SCRIPTURE

You are the body of Christ and parts of each other.

—1 Corinthians 12:27

VIDEO PRESENTATION

Notes:

Group Discussion Questions

1. Relationships Matter: Talk about the distinctions of a visitor versus a guest. How would you grade your church on its preparedness and expectation of receiving guests each week? Explain.

2. Review the steps below to moving a person from outsider to a follower of Christ. In your church, what is the intentional plan or process for following those steps?

Book Excerpt

From Outsider to Follower of Christ

Step One: From Outsider to Guest
      Phase One: Prayer
      Phase Two: Bridge Events
      Phase Three: Follow Up
Step Two: From Guest to Connected
Step Three: From Connected to Disciple
Step Four: From Disciple to Ambassador or Missionary

—*Get Their Name*, pp. 94–102

3. Leadership Matters: How does one go about becoming a leader in your congregation? What is the discernment process? What is the equipping process? What is the intentional process to raise up new leaders?

4. What is the intentional process of strategic ministry planning each year to align the ministries of the church with the mission, vision, and core values? What steps are missing? What are areas of needed improvement?

5. Building Matters: How guest friendly is your building? What works well? What needs improvement? What steps would you recommend? Who will take those steps?

6. If your church website is the first impression of your church, what kind of an impression are you making? How is your social media presence? What is working well? What needs to be improved?

KEY TAKEAWAY

_____

_____

_____

_____

_____

_____

_____

_____

_____

_____

CLOSING PRAYER

Note: Each person will pray today. Have one person start and each person will pray for the person on their right. The last person to pray will pray for the person that started the prayer. If possible, make the prayer personal based on the conversation and input from that group member during today's session.

HOMEWORK

What are your next steps? How will you become more comfortable in sharing your faith story? How will you create opportunities to begin new relationships with new unchurched people? How will you be a part of your church preparing for and receiving guests each week?

Would your group like to continue to meet together, learn more, and begin practicing the reaching of new people? If so, we have just the tool to take you to the next level. An extended workbook is available by the same title published by Abingdon Press. This workbook goes into depth on each of the ten chapters from the book *Get Their Name*. It covers topics not covered in the four-week study. This is a perfect next step for those desiring to learn more, adapt, and reach new people.

QUESTIONS FOR PERSONAL REFLECTION

1. What did God reveal to you in this study?

2. What action steps is God asking you to take?

3. Who will hold you accountable for those next steps?